Two Poems

Previous Publications by by Mario Sampaolesi

Poetry

Cielo Primitivo (Sociedad Argentina de Escritores, 1981)
La Belleza de lo Lejano (Editorial Amaru, 1986)
La Lluvia sin Sombra (Ediciones La Guillotina, 1992)
El Honor es Mío (Editorial Vinciguerra, 1992)
Puntos de Colapso (Ediciones del Dock, 1999)
Miniaturas Eróticas (Alción Editora, 2003)
A la hora del té (Barataria Poesía, 2007)
Malvinas – poema (Ediciones del Dock, 2010)
El taller de Leo (Libros del Zorzal, 2013)

Novels

La vida es perfecta (Alción Editora, 2005)
Monet (Libros del Zorzal, 2011)

Translations

El Cementerio Marino by Paul Valéry (Ediciones La luna que, 1998)
El monje loco está de regreso, a selection of poems by Ryokan
(Barataria, 1993)
Poemas de la Montaña Esmeralda, a selection of poems by Ryokan
(Nahuel Cerrutti Carol, Spain 2012)

Two Poems:

Malvinas
&
Points of Collapse

Mario Sampaolesi

Translated by
Ian Taylor

Shearsman Books

First published in the United Kingdom in 2013 by
Shearsman Books
50 Westons Hill Drive
Emersons Green
Bristol
BS16 7DF

Shearsman Books Ltd Registered Office
30–31 St. James Place, Mangotsfield, Bristol BS16 9JB
(this address not for correspondence)

www.shearsman.com

ISBN 978-1-84861-267-9

ACKNOWLEDGEMENTS
'Puntos de colapso' was first published by
Ediciones del Dock, Buenos Aires, 1999.
'Malvinas' was first published by
Ediciones del Dock, Buenos Aires, 2009.

Earlier versions of extracts from the 'Points of Collapse'
translation appeared in the magazine *Intimacy*.

Contents

Malvinas

MALVINAS is a large fragmentary poem. Sometime after the end of the war the idea of writing about the islands came to me quite clearly. But it wasn't long before the inevitable doubts crept in. In what way would the poem develop? How would I solve the various problems regarding its form and nature? For example, how could I avoid a patriotic tone, not fall into demagogy, ideological dogma and the like?

All these doubts (in reality, fears, as writing about the Malvinas carries several risks) seemed insoluble.

Then a few years passed with me seeming to have forgotten all about the idea, until around the middle of 2008, by which point all my doubts seemed to have resolved themselves. There was a sense of things having finally come together and the poem suddenly sprang into being.

It consisted of three voices: one anti-epic, one geographic and one subjective. The first encompasses the real and imaginary events of the poem; the second refers to the physical characteristics of the island and the third is that of a soldier-persona who returns to these islands twenty years after the war.

I was interested in this mosaic play, this play of scenes; I was, and remain, interested in the secret relationships that established themselves among the various fragments.

Not to mention the way certain narrative elements irrupted into the text.

M.S.

Malouines Soledad Falklands Borbón
Gran Malvina Trinidad Pelada Sebaldes
San José Bouganville Malvinas No
Malouines No Falklands Goicochea
Del Pasaje No Falklands No Malouines
Malvinas Borbón Soledad No Malouines
San Rafael Pelada Bouganville Malvinas
Gran Malvina Leones Marinos Soledad
San Rafael No Falklands Trinidad Soledad
Sebaldes Malvinas Sebaldes Goicochea
Soledad San Rafael Malvinas Borbón San
Rafael Trinidad Bouganville De los Leones
Marinos Aguila No Malouines Sebaldes
San Rafael No Falklands Goicochea
Malvinas Malvinas Malvinas

DEMOLITIONS: mortars impact upon wounded peat, upon trenches filled with boys smeared with the burning mire of war: sharp claws cut furrows across the small men's faces contorted with fear, touch down upon the terror of a fragmented terra firma, trepanned and smoking beneath the Malvinas sky; this grey and misty sky is created by the ascension of so much useless death, the futility of death erodes the clouds, the rotting steamroller clouds weigh upon the kelpers, upon the Brits, upon the Argies: each one dragging their innocent flesh over the tundra while being gnawed by the bite of an enormous fraud;

the ferocious portrait of the Queen, the dense, solemn granite bulk of the Military Fatherland collapses onto their shoulders, their backs; the marble shroud of sacrifice flattens their stooped silhouettes; the Holy Nation, the Holy Empire sacrifice these men at the altar of Righteousness and of Honour, these bleeding, bruised and bruising lads running zigzag like rabbits through the burning shrapnel tracers.

HE SENSES life when he hears the maddened calls of marine birds amid the crags; when he walks on rivers of stone carpeted with murmurs of water and fossil remains; painful clippings from his past appear reproduced in groups of damp, hermetic tussocks: scattered over the plain, they make this people-less planet visible.

He stops and suddenly realises just how far he was—until that scenic revelation—from the very notion of fulfilment; how remote —rupture of progress, fractured inertia— from that initiating act, from that beat that resembled a spark between the fog and the smoke.

The possibility of a reunion with a past that he wants he wanted to forget arises in the imaginary shape of a toboggan lying flattened where he slides, where he allows that body and himself to slide; he falls into the superficial depth of his image, towards the recognition of these bushes—"holy, holy," he murmurs as he caresses them—that seem to form a new instance of his soul.

He spots a clearing in the bushes, a possible oasis of purity, and stoops to make his way through the reed bed, then remains immobile in this space.

The wind is overwhelming, shaking him out of his impassivity; the screeching and rasping of distant sounds, of screams from the past, permeate the air; like metal scraping against a windowpane.

NOTHING REMAINS: the dim certainty of a dawn attack and fingers rhythmically stroking the barrel of a gun; fingers trembling with cold running their filthy calloused flesh over dull metal; dull grey metal caressed by words, gently brushed by murmurs from the mouths of boys; their ferric phonemes in stark relief against the shuddering night air, beneath the luminous zones of the flares.

In the suffering ditches small men exchange rumours under the protection of a shield of mist, safe behind the congealed damp of the islands; disturbances mounds orders retches astride silence, spasms beneath the mortal dome of bravery, of animal honour fleeing the scene by frog hops.

(TO HAVE NOTHING, to desire nothing, to be without before or after, to observe the flux of emotions, of memories, of thoughts; to feel immobile and remain so, without thinking, thinking from the depths of non-thought, to contemplate the maelstrom of events, to let them happen and forget them; to forget everything, to become empty, amnesiac, the gaze focussed beyond seeing and beyond this life that ceases to be a dream, that is not even a dream.)

And the ex-soldier, the ex-man, hears the savage murmur of vegetation rustling in the wind; he sees the marine birds' footprints, their various paths across the stones; he sees the frosty ground, a few drops hanging from

*the leaves above the tussocks; he feels in his
own flesh the albatross' beak as it pecks at
the silvery remains of a fish, devouring it in
bloody segments; he sees the clouds' capricious
sketches, their skittery movements; he sees the
wet and yellowy moss rotting upon older moss
long rotted and still rotting upon the peat; he
watches a seal's corpse disintegrate, its flesh
spreading towards him, transforming into a
writhing, slithering orgy of maggots; he hears
the wet slobbery buzzing of this seething mass;
he makes out, a few metres away, seagulls,
cormorants, plovers and kelp geese flapping
their wings, hunting, defecating, pecking,
cawing.*

Everything is the same forest.

THE MALVINAS ISLANDS form part of an archipelago situated in the South Atlantic Ocean.

They are roughly 550km from the entrance to the Magellan Straits and comprise more than one hundred islands, the largest of which are Soledad and Gran Malvina.

The former has a surface area of 4,353km^2 and the latter 6,307km^2.

Rugged plains with rocky outcrops are the territories' predominant features.

Between April and June 1982 1,847 people were wounded there.

Between April and June 1982 907 people died there.

FOUR STAKES driven into the black and red soil of the Malvinas.

Wrists swollen by restraints, taut rope, bits of leather (the young lad lies staked just like the small fort gauchos back in 1870), ankle bones visible in the gaping wound of the same old story.

The defenceless body with its face to the stars forms an X; easily discernible from the sky as an olive green letter on the black, sometimes red, Malvinas soil.

The man watches the stars, feels the cold metal sheet of the night weigh upon him, flatten and lacerate him; he trembles there, the ignored one, the one dying of disgust and fear.

Why him?

The drenching dew covers him, his pale, innocent flesh wounded by cruelty, rotting with each passing second, bleeding from the belt blow dealt by his countryman and shot by English bastards.

What exactly are they all doing there?

The earth receives him, the earth watered by the howls of innocent men. The cowardice and heroism of the young men produce roars that protect the mist perforated by projectiles, illuminated from within by flares, by fury, by terror, by the sharp crosses of the bayonets on the bullet-riddled manure of betrayal.

The Argentinian, the Argie, lies staked to the black-red Malvinas soil; he sees the sky, he sees the stars, he sees a fragment of the infinite.

But he'll never reach them.

*BLINKING: a flickering concealment prod-
uced upon the material of the eye, an instant
that could be said to resemble the life of a
cell, a space of time that is both negligible
and infinite; the moment in which the gaze
is extinguished beneath the weightlessness of a
small piece of skin, beneath the simultaneous
movement of eyelashes, barely a wound upon
vision (closure of eyelids) that is instantly
healed.*

*Veiling of the idea that strains towards the
surface, that strains to break away from that
eye, from that uncontrollable movement like
curtains closing: the possibility of distortion.*

*The gaze changes with each blink; consc-
iousness, daydreams and senses made flesh.*

Intermittently perceived, the vacillation to which it is subjected makes it difficult to capture the full complexity of reality.

With each passage of time some event goes unregistered.

The eyelids fall: at the point of greatest subtlety the outside world mutates and there occurs that which the gaze misses: in that uncontrolled space other realities develop, life continues its movement of expansion and contraction and the events unfurl without any possibility of us witnessing or even suspecting them; in that precise moment an insect may have died, the wind may have modified the shape of a stone, the clouds' shadows may have marked another area of pastureland.

A FEW MOUNTAIN RANGES cover the two main islands and stretch towards the outlying archipelagos. Like all old mountains—these date back to the Palaeozoic—they are low and generally rounded, though the odd fault has made them rugged in certain parts.

In Soledad the rocky formations extend from the bay of La Anunciación and stretch in a westerly direction towards San Carlos Straits.

They reach a height of 685 metres.

This phenomenon is repeated in Gran Malvina.

The plain, nevertheless, remains the dominant feature.

In Darwin, on a sunny, clear day, hundreds of white crosses sparkle in rows.

HE REMAINS sat in that clearing—with no possibility of Ariadne's thread—within the tussocks. An over-abundance of vegetation on all sides. He looks at the shrubs, observes his surroundings. He is certain that he has captured and stored within him the entire scene.

But what is happening in that which he does not see? What goes on around him when he closes his eyes? What disappears? What is lost? And how much does he really see of the landscape as he contemplates it?

And just how much of the visible remains invisible to the eye, to the gaze?

For even that which he sees may not be the whole but may instead just be the surface of a much deeper space, like a cavity that shows only its flat veneer, like the way you see only the front of a tunnel.

The green of the surrounding pasture-lands conceals this cavity, although the green is itself this cavity, stretched who knows how far, part of a whole whose presence is defined by fragments, by particularities.

And it is in this very spot that the ex-soldier, the ex-man, wishes to remain.

(As reality is fragmentary, all that we recall of a face is an expression, of a body a movement, of a smile the folds at the corners of the lips, of a landscape the impression of silence, and out of all other possibilities it is these pieces that we use to construct our own vision, an image that reproduces our internal image.

But what exactly is that internal image?)

"DIG A WELL, get digging, you son of a bitch; pick up that crappy little stick and scrape out that black Malvinas soil; dig, I said dig, you moron, and then if you want to stay alive you'd better climb into that hole 'cos the Gurkhas are coming."

The Gurkhas are coming and I'm alone on this freezing night, ploughed through by the blinding bright shrapnel projectiles; the mortars are getting closer and closer and I don't want to die here, far away from everything in the icy night of the islands, dazzled by the flares' shards as bright as the sun, herded here like cattle because I'm an Argentinian, but I don't want to die and it's so cold, and the Gurkhas are coming, they come crawling over the ever-black soil of the Malvinas, they are coming for me.

And I can feel them getting closer.

The NCOs say that after killing their enemies they eat their hearts, they'll eat this Argentinian heart that I feel beating in my chest right now, that beating heart will be torn to bits and then mashed between the Gurkhas' teeth, my Argentinian heart swallowed into the British stomachs of the Gurkhas, the blood of my sky blue and white heart will mix with their blood and our pasts with their burdens of pain and secrets will merge with each pulse, each beat.

I am all alone this night and I want to go home, I desperately want to go home before they eat my heart, my heart that feels so much love for this black soil, this soon to be black and red soil of the Malvinas.

But I can't go, I can't leave this spot, this deep hole that I dug with my little stick, this earth I scraped out with my fingers I could barely move with the cold, this muddy peat that I flattened and battered down with kicks from my frost-soaked walking boots, everything wet with the mutant mists of the islands.

Better to stay and meet my destiny, or whatever it was the captain said, but I miss my home and I can't see even though everything is fatally bright and the Gurkhas are coming.

But maybe just one of them, with the passage of time, who knows, the little pieces, the little morsels, the liquid shreds of my heart will maybe change just one of them.

THE WIND AND THE RAIN seem to be the only things permanent on the islands. Which explains why the landscape is so bereft of trees while shrubs and grasses spread everywhere in clumps and thickets. In the summer this vegetation is greyish green; in the winter it turns a yellowish colour.

The biological definition for this landscape is 'shrubby steppe'.

Another thing that grows on the islands is the tussock, which is the archetypal plant of the Malvinas and can grow up to three metres in height. These tussocks—similar to reeds—are highly coveted as food for livestock.

There are dense forests of these grasses throughout the islands, with seals and penguins making their home among them.

When the tourists come to visit they disembark from luxury cruisers and head straight for the pubs in Port Stanley.

There the kelpers tell them stories from the war, fill them in on where the minefields are and show them a few minor souvenirs: a handful of ammunition rounds left by the Argentine Army, bits of uniform, a few helmets.

Fixed to the wall with drawing pins is a large display of photographs—well thumbed and fading—of smiling young men.

NATURE converges there, at that extra-
ordinary point where the body is part of the
whole, where the spirit recognises anew the
inconstant essence of being.
Beneath the earth and the sky there are
obscure signs.
He is now able to clearly distinguish them,
he sees them seep through the cold of the
confining shadows of furtive regions; by deep
contemplation, he begins to recognise in this
landscape the visual representation of the soul.
He identifies life with a shadowy element in
which desire multiplies, and with the portion
of light that can be found in all things.
And the feeling of compassion for man makes
him the same as the others, and he falls silent

before the view of heaven, before the sudden revelation of the existence of a language of heaven, of a language created by the search for heaven.

He falls silent before the magnitude of this language and its possibility of escape, and the feeling of compassion for man makes him the same as the others, makes him one with the plain, makes him one with the immoderation of light when it passes through his matter, through the weak substance of his matter that also passes through every other form that surrounds him; for this fullness resides deep within him and he feels it vibrate like the taut string of an instrument whose music would make wild animals human.

And the feeling of compassion for man invades him, and completes him: he remains sat in the centre of the small tussock forest and it pierces

*him, tearing inside him with wild ferocity:
the freezing Malvinas wind paralyses his
face, enters though pores, perforates his skin;
he feels it filtering through his blood, mixing
with it, he feels it inflaming his blood with
the purity of its impulse and with its dense,
compacted texture, this mixture that may also
be solar, that he receives like an offering, that
moves, disturbs, intimidates: this coursing of
the wind through his insides, this lodging of
the wind in his blood and then throughout
his organs.*

*He can feel it running through his liver, his
pancreas, his stomach, his lungs, and feels it
freezing the slow beating of his heart.*

*He sits, immobile, bolt upright in the centre
of his own circle, equidistant from all the
different parts of his life: in front of him the
various points of his future; behind him the*

various points of his past. To each side of him the here and the now: a line of alephs resembling the horizon, a line along which he will slide.

THE FAUNA of the Malvinas belongs to the Patagonian zoogeological region, although there are also a few species peculiar to the islands' own continental zone. The variety of birds, both terrestrial and aquatic, is extraordinary. These consist of several species and fall into two categories:

a) Flying: there are petrels, albatrosses, gulls, cormorants, cape pigeons, white-tailed eagles, terns etc.

b) Non-flying: the most distinctive include the Kelp Goose (algae eaters), the Ruddy Duck (quite damaging to pasturelands and in danger of extinction), the Falkland Steamer Duck (a heavy marine duck that is exclusive to the archipelago), the Flying Steamer Duck (so called because of its lack of

speed and because it makes a noise like
that of a running motor) etc.

During the war a section of the islands'
fauna died.
During the war a section of the islands'
flora died.
The land and the sea were wounded by the
bombardments.

"Everything has feelings" —Pythagoras.

THE BRITISH MORTARS FALL shrill and heavy on the ingenuous Malvinas peat, on the hurt, hurting bodies of the little men flattened beneath a cloudy sky, beneath the steely, bestialized, illuminating opaque clouds of their sacrifice.

Hands and feet freeze in the ice and frost, aching and swelling to breaking point, smashing apart, bits of fingers, stalactites, standing out against the black and red Malvinas soil; they signal the impunity of plunder, the treachery behind all the militarist rhetoric.

The men plaster themselves flat against the walls of the foxholes, desperate to blend in with the heraldic Malvinas peat, seeking protection from the boiling metal that would evaporate them.

The English advance to kill them.

But not everything is paralysed by the fear of death: from amidst the shining lights of bombardment there appears the implacable monster of murder personified: loading the rifle, taking aim at the indistinct figure that approaches, at the unknown man who approaches, at this other man as alone as anyone, this other man also loved, hated, intelligent, stupid, kind, foolish, brilliant etc, this other human being who howled and howls, he too feeling fear, hatred, disgust, courage, thinking about killing another man, killing some unknown man who is a son, lover, brother, father, husband; the heavy burden of murder drags down the military orders, the patriotic symbols, drags them down to this place where they crawl through the peat petrified with the inevitability of the crime, forced to act upon a decision obeying which will leave them cast out from humanity, they are all frozen here.

Over the remains of mutilation, over the piled-up corpses falls the shadow of combat, the solitude of combat, the lonely cries.

THE KITE *flies above the stern.*
To the left. To the right.
It goes, went, will go against the wind.
Inflated by the wind, it floats above the white
wake that opens behind the boat. The scarlet
kite, the Tibetan kite swinging back and forth
between the sky and the sea, perpendicular to
the spray, floating further and further from
the sailboat's stern, an extravagant and
monstrous bird, its shadow brushes the fish's
fins, modifies the colouring of certain parts of
the swell.
The kite flies in the distance, between the sky,
sea and sailboat; an object different from and
yet somehow the same as that other object,
the sailboat, which is also flying though
upon the swell, upon the Prussian blue mass
of the sea, the white sailboat with a solitary
man standing at the rudder, a metaphysical

*painting, the white sailboat set against that
density, different from and yet identical to
the kite, that crimson banner simultaneously
static and flaming against the immaterial sky,
upon that cloudless blue; a red blaze flying
over the scene.*

*It is, will perhaps be youth fluttering; the
remains of those years, the spoils cutting
like thorns, like bites: the terrible time of
his youth pursues him, alcoholic, drugged,
dazed, in spite of his desire to distance himself
from those days, in spite of his determination
to bury in some unknown land that heavy
burden on his shoulders, that load it takes
him every ounce of strength in his body to
carry; but he bends, he stoops; he drags the
enormous mass of that distant time and now
sees it in that kite flying in the distance, tied to
a boat's stern by a thin piece of string; so easy*

41

to free himself from his sins, his past, so simple
to throw them overboard like waste, so sweet
to suddenly cut oneself off from pain like this;
a sharp scraping of the knife against the rope,
a gradual fraying of the rope and with it the
erosion of barbarism, the string thinner and
thinner, becoming one with reality, with that
past growing weaker and weaker, a barely
audible tone, memories fading in and out
with the scraping of the blade against the rope,
the amputation of the war's conflagration
weighing on his shoulders all these years,
oppressive and terrifying like a burden of acid
and steel, then this simple act of cutting the
thin umbilical cord connected to the past, a
barely visible line in the distance, a line of
reference, a curve, vulnerable to gusts of wind,
a line stretched to the sky and to the horizon,
connecting the loathsome kite with the whole
of life in the same way his youth is connected

to this moment, to this solitary journey that he is undertaking to free himself from what he does not have, to rid himself of what he has lost, to feel the emptiness he feels every day of his life, to distance himself from the viruses of a past that he wants to forget, that he wishes had never happened; a few steps taken in the wrong direction, an entrance into a tunnel via the path least travelled, a move towards a dangerous situation.

All of a sudden he's right there, in the sailboat. He watches the kite swing towards one and then another side of life, sees it sway to the rhythm of the blade, oscillating like a scarlet representation of every doubt, every weakness. With each movement over the cord the knife cuts away the daily poisons of hatred, reproach and malice; it cuts away the fear associated with concealment (that vast shadowy place known to no one).

It is also witness to a light trembling, like the prelude to full redemption: a few cold drops splashed from the sea dampen the man's face, falling upon it with the same rhythm as the rain when he fired into the windows of the family home, with the exact same rhythm as the shrapnel beating against the soil of the trench: that terrible life flies over him in that scarlet kite, flies over him monstrously in that Tibetan kite; he watches it rise, watches it undulate obliquely above that moment, above the percussion of that instant.

The scene contains a column of light falling between two clouds, a newborn dolphin's cry of alarm, the portion of air sealed within the curve of a wave and a red stain, outside of the sky, of the ocean, free.

DISTINCTIVE AMONG the marine mammals is the South American Fur Seal, a native of the Malvinas that is also known as the Southern Fur Seal. This reproduces at a few post stations. It is between 1.4 and 2 metres in height and its weight fluctuates between 50 and 160kg.

Sea leopards (ferocious carnivores who feed on penguins, with devastating effects upon their numbers), sea lions, seals and elephant seals are not native to the islands but take up temporary residence there while migrating to or from the Antarctic.

The male Southern Elephant Seal possesses a short trunk that acts as a resonating chamber for making its roar more powerful.

At various points around the islands can be found nature observatories from which these animal colonies are studied.

Government representatives say that they contribute to a greater understanding and conservation of the species.

In the year 1820 North American and English fishing boats arrived at the islands with notices from their governments authorizing the hunting of seals.

The men clambered out of their boats armed with sticks.

This is how they hunted, with blows from sticks.

The dense colonies of these animals were reduced to prey.

THE EX-SOLDIER throws scraps of meat to the seals, bits of food expelled from his own body, from his skin, from the feverishly burning body thrown into a series of rigid contortions by the effort of relinquishing them, of ridding himself of these parts of his life that were shaped by illusion, by the expectation of an eternally unyieldable love.

He picks them out of a pile that he had kept locked away in an enormous ancient wooden chest, a chest he would often hide inside during his childhood, the only place where he felt safe, a refuge for him to hide and protect the objects most precious to him.

(Submerged in that darkness, on his knees, hunched up, he would hear his own panting breath; there would also be the odd cold night

when he could see his breath in whirling
clouds against the light that filtered in as
he held the chest lid slightly open: this also
enabled him to watch his mother move about
and listen to muffled conversation and the
fearsome steps of his father.)

SINCE TIME IMMEMORIAL four classes of penguin have been observed on the Malvinas: the King, the Gentoo, the Western Rockhopper and the Magellanic Penguin.

The King Penguin is the largest among those that inhabit the islands and the second largest among all penguins: only the Emperor Penguin is larger.

The Gentoo Penguin has a red or orangey beak and a sort of white cap that stretches from one eye to the other on an otherwise black head.

At around sixty centimetres in height, the Western Rockhopper is smaller than the Gentoo. Its head is adorned with two yellowish crests (hence its name in Spanish: *el pingüino de penachos amarillos*) stretching from the beak area at both sides.

The Magellanic Penguin is a little taller at seventy centimetres. Its beak is a dark grey colour while its head is mostly black with a U-shaped white band.

The sea leopard represents the main predator for penguins, with his voracious attacks placing entire colonies in danger.
Killer whales and sharks also sometimes attack them.
However, neither the skin nor meat of penguins has any value for man.
This fact increases the penguin's chances of survival.

VORACITY, yes, but an inverse voracity: it never was but is and will be the axis of his life: instead of swallowing, of assimilating, amassing, he now expels, vomits, dredges up from deep within himself everything that he has brought here to be turned into shadow, all those experiences that were becoming flesh, liver, trachea, kidney, oesophagus, heart, blood; everything in him that was pain and anguish; everything that constituted his circulatory system, his respiratory system, his nervous system: the framework of his being trembles at the certainty of loss, of dissolution, of that situation akin to the void, to oblivion. Leprosy.

But he still cannot shake his belief in this strength, in this sensation of finality, of

breathlessness, of crucifixion, of the forming
of currents, of wind.
He believes in this possibility of liberation, of
purification.
And now the light, extremely light caress of
his mother returns to pass over his skin once
more, but not without consequences: it rusts
his emotions, leaves a sea wake, the fluttering
and cawing of gulls on the spume, the pecking
for fish on the sea's surface.
They are signs adrift of a past that expels him,
a non-refuge (the same symbol but not the
same object: that large chest will be destroyed,
split apart by frenzied axe blows, each blow
destroying the secret scenes of a child struck
dumb, the victim, prey, of his father's hunts;
each blow eliminating the putrid snacks that
nourished him throughout his youth), a non-
refuge, he repeats, a place of disprotection from
which to transform the insult, from which to
illuminate the horror.

THE PEAT is a filthy, watery sponge.

Everything sinks into it.

It absorbs everything.

The little man, the young soldier, is thrown and flattened against this cold, floating darkness.

He tries to dissolve himself in this aquatic surface that yields so easily to him while awaiting the attack, while the wind tears across the Malvinas plain.

He struggles against the mist hanging in the air, its liquid density weighing upon his body.

His feet, hands, arms and legs are frozen, his face is several layers of frost, the gun an iceberg mass of grey metal, while the wind tears across the plain, while the leaden clouds load up on more rain, preparing for the deluge: a flood without mercy, leaving no possibility for escape or shelter.

The young man is hoping that the English come soon, he is waiting for them to come and kill him.

He is alone like all the others scattered about, all buried in their foxholes; every one of them waiting for the bullet.

After the gunshot rings out the quiet calm returns, then the projectile finds its target in the body, passes through the raincoat stiff with dirt, the jacket, the pullover that someone knitted in Buenos Aires before it somehow found its way to this place, the work shirt, the diary pages, the vest, the bullet passes without resistance through the young soldier's clothes, penetrates the skin, explodes in the blood, in the flesh, splits the bone, shatters it, enters the lung, the English bullet pierces the lung in the infinite solitude of the Malvinas plain.

But it's not just his body it penetrates, it also passes through his memories of home, of his mother, his brother, his girlfriend, his friends, his hometown; the bullet explodes inside the very essence of the man, the Argie, the young soldier who won't surrender, the little guy who despite not being able to be, despite not wanting to be, despite not having wanted to be is now a hero.

And he dies.

And everything that we didn't know, everything that we didn't want to know, everything we never imagined expands like lead in his stomach.

THERE WAS ONCE a great abundance of cetaceans in the waters of the Malvinas.

They chose this region because of the vast quantities of krill in these waters, a crustacean of high nutritional value that also happens to be their favourite food.

The blue whale is the largest living animal; towards the end of the nineteenth century tens of thousands of these whales populated the Southern and Antarctic Oceans.

Now there are just a few hundred of them left as they face almost certain extinction.

European and Asian—mainly Japanese—fishermen plunder the South Atlantic. Their ships simultaneously serve as factories

where the prey is immediately processed:
cut into pieces, canned, packaged.
Productivity – efficiency – business.
Packaging – design – marketing.
Within minutes of the beautiful creature
swimming elegant and free.

No control, no mercy.
No guilt.

THE EX-SOLDIER tries to rupture the fabric constructed by fear, by guilt; guilt, that figure forever behind him, that sound of footsteps, that pursuit through dark corridors, through secret passageways, through caves fled into when trying to escape from the false calls of so much egotism.

He feeds.

He feeds on that parasite, on the leftovers of his own pain, on the bloody and still-beating scraps of his bruised childhood, on the false offerings of a youth where the protective shield of love's caresses failed; where the steely defences fell at his feet, battered by blows from the iron spikes of betrayal, crushed by bombardments of resentment.

His former ego now lies among the remains
of that chest of wood and flesh and blood
and guts and punishments; it lies among the
pieces of a non-existent childhood, among the
splinters of a youth bullet-riddled with lies.
The ex-soldier uses an old stick to dig a deep
hole, a deep and narrow well in the red
Malvinas soil into which to throw everything
he once was, to bury everything he'll never be.
He lifts the body of the past, the other, raises
it above his head then hurls it deep into
that cavity, into the bosom of the earth;
bacteria, worms and rodents will gnaw away
at that skin and consume the flesh beneath
it; the former ego will be feasted upon and
swallowed by this ferocious blackness; he sees
the shape fall apart, the broken puppet shape
of a once living body; he sees how threads once
tense and animate now lie in a withered and

flaccid pile on the ground; he sees the material of the past disintegrate in that well where for just one moment there shone the influence of a clarity, the silver-plated purification of the stars.

And together with this fragmented figure containing his whole life up to that point, up to the end of the straight line he traces in front of himself, he also buries the volatile signs of the history created by his imagination; around him there remains nothing but photographs, love letters burned and still smouldering, the pages black with red borders, all lifted and stacked into a column by rising eddies of wind, obscured by clouds swiftly blocking the light of the moon.

No Malouines Soledad No Falklands
Gran Malvina Trinidad Pelada Sebaldes
Aguila   Bouganville Malvinas San Rafael
Goicochea Del Pasaje No Falklands No
Malouines Malvinas   Borbón   Soledad
No Malouines San   Rafael   Goicochea
Pelada   Malvinas   Gran   Malvina De
los Leones Marinos Äguila San Rafael
Del   Pasaje   No Falklands   Trinidad
Soledad Sebaldes   Malvinas   San   José
Sebaldes   Goicochea   Soledad
San   Rafael   Malvinas   Trinidad Aguila
Malvinas Borbón No Falklands   Pelada
No Malouines Sebaldes Del Pasaje No
Falklands No   Malvinas   No   Malvinas
No Malvinas No Malvinas No Malvinas

Points of Collapse

to my son Bernardo
to my sister Mabel
to my parents

It was will be a stillness apart from everything, deprived of everything: an upright posture separating itself from the concept of the other: it immerses itself in its identity, in its essence without language, without transcendence.

Only the final sense of the void; the rhythm of that void contains silence and with its power deflowers, tears petals away:

It provokes autumn, modifies the dawn.

The formation, the part, the whole, the identity, that which indicates and signals: they provoke.

For all its attractive instability, the exposure of flight still warns of the power latent within that flesh, within that density that resides would reside in some of the infinite forms of the created:

idea of satiety, of dispossession, of frequency.

There exists only the possibility of multiple combinations, encounters, points of collapse, explosions.

Wind: the stereophonic sound of the wind.
The wind is a howl.
Its gusts never cease inside my head.
It is piercing here in the mountains.
Brown
  white
        yellow
            blue.
All these colours are inside me.
They form my body, composing and decomposing it.
They become flags.
At the peak, at the highest point, there is a flag.

Delved into by clarity, the penumbra counters the light with obscure displacements; shudderings of a slavery, of a sentence carrying the possibility of touch, of encounter.

Harassments, intimacies, tunnels, damp solitary corners; walls on which names are deciphered will be deciphered like calls, like prayers.

Climbing a mountain isn't easy.
Above everything else one must be brave, more so
if the purpose of the climb is to take photographs.
It is also said that in the mountains one is closer
to God.
The air is purer, etc.
This must be true, as I feel that closeness.
When I stop and hear the wind,
I hear nothing but the wind.
When I flatten myself against the walls, I flatten
myself against nothing but the walls.
It must be true.
In the mountains one is closer to God.

I have reached a strange point on the mountain.
I don't recognise it.
I look at my watch. It says 2.11p.m.
I take the camera out.
I want to capture this place so as to calmly look at it later.
Without reliving this sensation of not recognising it.

Wind
　　　wind
　　　　　wind.
　　　　　　　　Snow.
The wind of snow.
　　　　　　　　　　The mountain.
I take one, two, ten steps upward.
I think I recognise it.
But I don't.
More and more wind and snow. Another mountain.
There is a moment in everyone's life when nothing
seems easy
　　　clean
　　　　　pure.

I won't come down just yet.

The explosion of the viscera refracts all death throes.

By the simple act of observing, all understanding can be attained.

In the glare of pain, the sum of every drop of blood, of every particle of matter, will transform the conception of temporary and permanent being via that of contemplation and forgetting.

The passive will thus connect with an unexplored landscape; lashed by repentance and ecstasy.

The stillness was will be unconquerable.

I feel the cold.
I breathe and feel the cold.
Its glass needles scrape at my lungs.
I go back the same way I came. I intend to return to the cave I saw yesterday and was afraid to enter. I must be strong, I tell myself. I must enter and stay there.
Take photographs.
I feel the cold.
I drink the light to warm myself up.

That kind of erosion disintegrates would disintegrate together with the voice, the cry; the howl will come would come from the well, from that fenced-in pain: that elastic membrane falling like larva, like mist, upon all that it covers.
Manic hope.

That will's pulsations form the vague appearance of some secret. And yet a cry, an agitation, occurs in the stillness: frozen in its own movement, the pendulum becomes incapable of all immobility. The idea of stasis is now added to this aboriginal emotion of the whisper, of the murmur heard among leaves, among foliage.

It speaks of passions, of dispossessions, of searches and also of returns.

A storm is coming. I can feel it.
Nothing else could account for the different sound
of the wind, the flight of certain animals.
I am alone in the cave in front of the fire.
At night in the mountain there is only the cold and
the wind.
I hear the sound of the snow as it breaks against
the walls.
I perceive and do not perceive the void.

The storm has lasted two days so far.
Fortunately I managed to catch a strange, shaggy
creature.
To clean it I split it open.
I take photographs of its innards.
Many photographs of its innards.
I must never forget this moment.
Like an animal, I kill to survive.

Poisoned by certain appearances, solitude maintains its obsessive elements.

Its languors harbour discontinuous flowerings, beatings of lights amidst the shadows.

Tensed, they would display they display a roughness, a ruggedness that converts would convert signs and things into tremors and silenced fervours.

Everything ends up will end up hiding itself within continuity: oblivion extends its wall, its infinite ribbon of sinuous cement through a forest, a mountain chain, a jungle.

This sensation of hardness, of non-porosity, of a circle in motion, becomes oval; this form of non-spongy volume advances, occupying space after space, exceeding the limits of the one who in order to satisfy pleasure evolves :

then there will always be a process of rain, of disquiet, unease.

I cut my prey up into small, identical pieces.
I made a small cage out of branches and scraps of
wood.
I hung the meat on this cage to let it air.
Then I sat before the fire and watched the storm.
I just sat before the fire and watched the storm.
This too will pass, I told myself.

I hear the sound of the snow as it breaks against the stones.
In the mountains there is only the sound of the snow as it breaks against the stones.

To become absorbed, to blacken, emerging from certain key moments (like the movements of a swing) or from an uncertain light that has no memory of any place: to become a furrow, a wake, the imaginary route left by the passage of the clouds; to dream of the markings of desire: echoes, profanations.

I must leave the cave, I tell myself.
But first I will have to find a path.
I still do not know nor understand why I must first
find a path.
There is nowhere to go, no place to find, no city to
live in.
I am in the mountain and that is all, and the only
thing around me is the mountain.

I must find a path.

The rupture is a mirror. Its weight of a fragrance, of a feather's fall, modifies the history of an encounter: the dawn defeated by nausea, by the stripping away of so many dreams, of so much abandonment.

The strangeness of this landscape gains
nourishment from the fatal; it survives in a
sequence repeated day after day: it possesses an
emotional charge that, at its most dangerous,
forms part of despair. Because it has left behind
precipice after precipice after precipice and so
on.

The waste of life then turns into the culmination
of old age: terrifying, it clamours for its place of
happiness, its snowy refuge.

But in the hidden recesses of every pleasure there exists an identity. It is hidden and little by little disappears.
One lives on losses, on events (each following the other like fragments of a musical refrain).
Disharmonies, displacements prevail would prevail over that idea of happiness crouching in the blood:
if there had only been promises broken by hell, their possibility of paradise aborted by lack of depth, by extremes without limits, by the absence of love.

I hear the sound of the night as it breaks against the mountain.

I imagine the hardness of the blow, the splash of geometrical shadows, of black, sharp, cutting particles.

I think of my life before now and it seems distant and absurd.

Absurd and distant.

The night, the wind, they break against the mountain.

The storm comes to an end.
Half-frozen, I go out and try to warm myself
beneath the day's tubercular sun.
In spite of the cold I contemplate the landscape.
I take photographs.
I jump up and down.
You were always the same, I say to myself.
You still believe in the immutable.

Six-day beard.
Cold.
Six-day smell.
Cold.
I abandon the 'comfort' of the cave.
The meteorological signs confirm that the worst has
passed.
In my life too the worst has passed.
I know this because in front of me the snowflakes
fall white
*   and fleeting.*

Form reproduces the cry from the depths from the precipice. The depths materialise their undesired structure, camouflaged, hidden by necessity, by fear.
The point of encounter is collapse.

The dawning of a new situation clears the snow from the stage where the drama unfolds.

Every text reproduces living sensations. Every living sensation is transmuted or is capable of being transmuted into text.

It is oblivion.

As I advance the landscape retreats.
As I ascend part of the mountain descends.
Whenever I shout the mountain falls silent.
When I am silent I hear the landscape.
This is true and at the same time not true.

Disturbances, falls, decoys,
crossroads: sensations, objects and locations
of a displacement, an invasion: the hours too
resemble grindings, bastard omnipotences,
paranoiac films, US citizens drinking alone in
hotel rooms (Sunset Boulevard).

Midday.

The breath's vapour, the pure as pure blue of a cloudless sky, the polished yellow of the sun and the large black golden-gloved figure above the snow create a strange tableau vivant.

Though I am in the mountain the mountain is beyond me.
The mountain is the mountain.
And its memory will remain within me.
But the memory of the mountain is not the mountain.
This happens because though we may share the same space we remain different.
I am in the mountain.
The mountain is beyond me.

Every once in a while life empties out its contents. The flux comes to a halt and one is able to make out Hell *(hell is really on earth —Rimbaud)*, caught up in that twilight that is the image of our decadence, the flowering of an abstract pus: it perforates, penetrates, contaminates.

Every search culminates in misapprehension, every loss ends in growth, in expansion, the generation of space.

Every point of collapse evolves into an explosion, and from explosion into expansion (an increase in understanding, tolerance and patience).

Blurred images, outlines, sinuosities, fire.

The thaw will soon be here.
This is heralded by a finite, crystalline streamer of
water.
I kneel down and start emptying out my rucksack.
Tin plate and cup, plastic and metal cutlery, pieces
of chocolate wrapped in cellophane, a book I have
no intention of reading, a spare pair of gloves, etc.
The wind crystallises a few stones dampened by the
water running down the mountain slope.
I stand up.
I decide to leave everything here.
The rucksack included.

The hammering in the depths transcends an opacity: it clarifies, creates transparency.
Darkness becomes luminous when it is a product of an immersion. The truly deep is difficult to comprehend.
This must be why ease is contrary to growth.
And is deceitful.

Consummation of dreams, submission to a contact, to a collapse.

Provocation of spaces, of openings, of silences.

The solitary mania of stagnant water, odorous and putrid where contagion breeds.

Fevers, visions, typhus: the pink, flaky skin of the hermaphrodite, his blind eye.

A hexagonal surface, a collection of samples, a zoo.

I sit facing the stone.
In the silence of nature I just sit with my face to
the stone.
I do not contemplate
        nor think
                nor speak
                        nor listen.
I do not move.
Each instant resembles a drop of water that grows
smaller as it quickly evaporates on burning sand.
I understand its disappearance.

Such is this moment, and the next, and the next.

The mist promises mystery, dreams, distance.
An eroticisation brought about by its secrets,
forms that last throughout time and emotional
shifts.
Bones, poems, paintings, cities: constructions of
despair, scraps.

Something strays from the mind: a thought or just the sensation of having thought. That impression of reliving certain events would maintain its connection with oblivion (the final mercy would be memory, memory as a secret refuge against loss.)

(This accumulation that is memory, if it lasts it would disrupt it disrupts an order, would destroy it destroys all organisation.)

How is it possible to love the vision of the corpse eaten by worms? How love the vision of diseases coagulating all movements? How love the contemplation of that which is falling apart? Someone will kiss our pain.

The breath's vapour, the pure as pure blue of a cloudless sky, the polished yellow of the sun and the large black figure wearing golden gloves, all combine to create a strange tableau vivant.

I would like the spirit of this landscape to stay like this for ever.

Disparity of objects, of observations; the concrete passageway into which one fears to tread, to fall, to slide along.

(The idea of a continuation of life would demonstrate the falling of the leaves, the red splendour of the blaze, the hardness of the mountain.)

Submission to the empire of sensations, the mounds flattened by the lake's reflection; the hanging suspense of a trapeze artist's carefully planned trajectory...

The cumulus of the void deteriorates will deteriorate throughout its history; it offers will offer a new condition to the tired spinning of the distaff, to the burning mill firmly embedded in the night.

To await the freshness of pleasure, the advent of
a magnificent dream.

Crepuscular, stoical suffering, enriched by the vicissitudes of impulses, desires, by the remains of those feelings that pile up like waste; from this point pain will emigrate emigrates, leaving behind a hollow, an exhalation of absence, an unfulfilled need that will subsequently die of its own atrophy: its neurotic asphyxia coughing up a black and bitter pus made salty by metamorphosis, by the splitting of pain.

To suddenly understand the bloody cracks of the earth, its forests.

I see

    I listen

        I breathe.

I look at the rocks and discover landscapes, figures, animals, shapes.

Everything was and was not always there; but never before have I been able to perceive it, nor stop perceiving it.

I see

    I breathe

        I listen.

Therein lies the existence of the other.

Before my eyes the snowflakes crisscross as they fall
  white
      fleeting.

There is a moment in life in which everything seems easy
      clean
          pure.
The day
      the wind
          break against the mountain.

The earth is expected to bring forth a shoot, a germination, a life.

From the sky is expected a hope, an angel, an answer.

From the fire a descent, an intensity, a shadow.

From the water is expected a swaying, a flowing, a memory.

To see oneself as earth, sky, fire, water.

To become the other.

I go on small expeditions. I explore.
I take photographs.

Little by little the weather improves.
I have been here for many days.
Perfumes
       sounds
             colours I never noticed before
begin to invade me.
It's strange.
I always thought that I myself was the invader.
But the mountain grows and grows, growing larger
and larger inside me.
I take photographs.

Sinuosities, trajectories, crosses, encounters. These words come together in shelters, in paths, in passageways, in walls. Their secret routes confirm the possibility of their existing solely as an answer. Every answer is the result of a question. Every answer gives rise to a new question.

Words do not exist.

*What is dangerous about being in the mountains is
forgetting that one is in the mountains.
I think about this while adjusting my golden gloves,
checking the camera and walking to a shelter in
the rocks.
The mountain is stone and stone and stone.
The stone is the mountain.
This must be why it is as much a mountain inside
as outside.*

*When it is dark in the depths it is dark on the
surface.
When it is light in the depths it is light on the
surface.*

I look at the rocks and discover landscapes
                      figures
                               animals
                                         shapes.

But in the rocks there are no landscapes
                      figures
                               animals
                                         shapes.

In the rocks there are only rocks.

Like the golden crust of guilt, there emerges from its dark seat of honour this idea of desolation, of a hardened feeling beginning to crack.

Shakings, distortions: the very movements of a convulsion peeling off in strips: the howling of pigs submerged in the boiling waters of our desire.

Thou shalt not kill.

I must leave the cave, I tell myself.
But first I will have to find a path.
The cave is not a place.
But first I will have to find a path.

I must leave the path.

The mountain twists, curves back on itself.
Its view is of a wall, of emptiness.
As I ascend I imagine and as I imagine I remember,
and thus the ascension, the imaginary and the past
merge, each superimposing itself on the other.
Facing the stone I see the sky and this action has a
calming effect.
It is almost as if I were dead, but without the
tormenting idea of death.

(If by inverting the image I could fix the shock
of the sky against the outline of my silhouette, its
elastic sheets would adopt the shape of the force that
beats it and against which the sky

                                        comes apart.)

It rises, rises, a cloud of smoke.
It grows, grows, electric nature, love, turtle love.
Engendering the cruelty that never dies.

Fury, the racket of pages, of writings crackling like broken lights, like lies.

Could the hurricane love itself for no other reason than the sense of beauty possessed by its immense destructiveness.

Could the limpid, pure sky hate itself for no other reason than the disequilibrium surrounding every perfect landscape.

Calm, the tranquillity of respiration, the silence of serene readings like dark deities, like sirens.

When I ascend a part of the mountain ascends
with me.
When I shout the mountain shouts.
When I make no sound the mountain falls silent.

In the other there exists the other.

The day breaks against the mountain.
I hear the hardness of the blow, imagine the splash
of its clarity, its geometrical particles, luminous,
sharp, cutting.
How to find light in shadow?
How find shadow in light?
For shadow is completely shadow and light
completely light.
For it is dark in the depths of darkness and
luminous in the depths of light.

Yet still there exists a darkness in light, a luminosity
in shadow.

Scattered objects, leftovers, nylon, polythene sachets full of blood, hypodermic needles: the vestal, sculpturally virgin and young, rubs herself against the apple tree in bloom. She ignores the naked man resting beneath the foliage. She ignores the serpent and the idea that a serpent could exist.

Pieces of burnt paper, the sound of a train passing over bridges, broken light bulbs, bits of wood and iron, computer cemeteries, the hypocrisy of a suffocating, perverted civilisation.

I love you Eve.

I stand before a large snow-covered crag.

At the bottom of the precipice is a pine coppice.

Nowadays avalanches occur quite frequently (thawing etc).

I shout.

AHOEEEEEE…AHHHHOOOOOEEEEEE…

I shout louder.

AAAAAAHHHHHHOOOOOOOOOEEEEEE

I aim my camera and shoot, snatching a photograph before the avalanche starts.

I change the lens…

I take photos while listening to the tremor, the roar.

The avalanche begins.

I shoot, shoot, shoot.

The avalanche slides headlong towards the void; it drags the pine coppice down with it for three thousand metres.

It buries it.

One by one the trees crack and snap.

Birds' eggs, insects, squirrels and other small animals unknown to myself must now lie wounded or dead.

I take panoramics and close-ups with the telephoto lens. Also a photo of the no longer snow-covered crag.

Thou shalt not kill, I tell myself.

I take photograph after photograph.
I seize each moment and fix it.
I place Polaroid beside Polaroid beside Polaroid
and so on.
Then I study them, remembering that day in its
entirety.

And thus another and another and another and
another.

This evening makes plain the impossibility of all action. Nothing can put right this state of desolation, of solstice, of nervation. In the calm is expected the irruption of the event. In the action is expected the arrival of the point of inertia.

It would be necessary to not intervene in the course of this space absorbed by time.

This evening sucked up by contemplation possesses the virtue of stripping the day of its relationship to flesh, to profit.

Reality moisturised by drizzles.

Totems.

Objectives mutate from the onset of desire.
Desire is mutated by objectives.
There exists an abandonment to routine.

The mountain contains me.

In spite of myself, of my atrocious egotism, of so much solitude with its ineffable weight, the mountain contains me.

Its sweet hardness opens up and takes me in, offering me shelter and nourishment.

I walk along the mountain as if along the body of a giant who supports me, offering me understanding and calm.

In spite of myself, of my atrocious egotism, of so much solitude with its ineffable weight.

I hear the sound of the snow as it breaks against the stones.
At night in the mountain there is only the sound of the snow breaking against the stones.

Crypt confessions; sealed mysteries, locks, ciphers of a key that would reveal will reveal the meaning of life, monoliths: he disfigures his face with a blade worked from marble.

He wounds himself in order not to think, not to dream.

The irritated veneer of his solitude moves in the dark like sails, with a texture like silk, like purple, getting soaked by the rain.

He dreams of sacred objects, of sexual devices, of stones made damp by treachery, of the beginning of all deformation.

Nature is the true nature of the mountain.
Nature is my true nature.
The mountain contains me.
I contain the mountain.
And yet the mountain is not myself.
And yet I am not the mountain.

Biographical Notes

MARIO SAMPAOLESI was born in Buenos Aires on the 16th of June 1955. He spent two years living in France between 1989 and 1991, and was the editor of the poetry magazine *Barataria* from 1993 to 2008. Since 2003 he has been running the Poetry Workshop at the National Library in Buenos Aires.

IAN TAYLOR was born in Liverpool, raised on the outskirts of Wigan, and after spells in Chatham, Leamington Spa, Leeds, Buenos Aires and Cardiff has lived in rural Dorset since 1997. He has had two books of prose and poetry published by Spectacular Diseases (*Ruins* and *Work Without Production / Mangled Machinery*), as well as appearing in the 1994 anthology from the same press. His works appeared in several magazines throughout the U.K., U.S.A. and Argentina in the 1990s and early 2000s, while his translation of Fernando Kofman's *Zarza remueve* was published as *The Flights of Zarza* by Arc Publications in 2008. Between 1997 and 2001 he edited the magazine *écorché*.

Lightning Source UK Ltd.
Milton Keynes UK
UKOW04f1324220913

217655UK00001B/23/P